ABC
Animal
RIDDLES

by **Susan Joyce**

illustrations by **Doug DuBosque**

Peel Productions, Inc.

Published by Peel Productions, Inc.
PO Box 546, Columbus NC 28722

http://peelbooks.com

Printed & bound in Hong Kong

L_____y of Congress
Cataloging-in-publication data

Joyce, Susan, 1945–
    ABC animal riddles / by Susan Joyce ; illustrations by
Doug DuBosque
        p.   cm.
    Summary: Rhyming alphabet-based riddles challenge
the reader to identify animals from clues, including
the first and last letter of the word.
    ISBN 0-939217-51-1 (alk. paper)
    1. Riddles, Juvenile.   [1. Riddles. 2. Animals. 3.
Alphabet.]   I. DuBosque, D. C., ill. II. Title.

PN6371.5.J677 1999
818'.5402--dc21   98-42518

a_t

I start with an A and end with a T.
My family lives
in a big colony.
We are ruled by a queen,
who is not often seen.
She lays eggs continuously.
Can you name me?

b_____r

My name has six letters.
It starts with a B.
With my very large teeth,
I can cut down a tree.
I build dams with a mix
of mud, stone and sticks.
I'm a rodent. I'm furry.
What can I be?

c _ _ _ l

I start with a C and end with an L.
I live in the desert,
a hard place to dwell.
When I'm feeding well,
my large hump will swell.
If I have two humps,
they swell as well.
I carry people,
or goods that they sell.
What am I? Can you tell?

d _ _ k

I start with a D and end with a K.
My flat bill is perfect
for dabbling all day.
To keep my feathers clean,
I preen and preen and preen.
I waddle when I walk.
I quack when I talk.
What's my name? Can you say?

e_____

My name has eight letters.
It starts with an E.
I live on the land,
and I'm big as can be.
My unusual nose
also works as a hose,
and a trumpet which blows.
Phe-oop-eiee! What can I be?

f_____y

I start with an F and end with a Y.
When it's light out, I hide.
When it grows dark, I fly.
I dance and flash my light—
five flashes, green and bright.
I let female beetles know
I'm watching for their glow.
What am I? Do you know?

g_____e

I start with a G and end with an E.
Spots cover my skin.
I'm a strange sight to see.
When my neck stretches high,
my head's in the sky.
I'm as tall as a tree.
Can you name me?

h_____s

I start with an H and end with an S.
My barrel-shaped body
is almost hairless.
I'm related to the pig,
but I'm really, REALLY BIG!
I swim and laze all day.
At night I graze away.
What am I? Can you say?

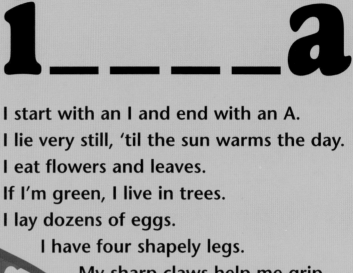

i_____a

I start with an I and end with an A.
I lie very still, 'til the sun warms the day.
I eat flowers and leaves.
If I'm green, I live in trees.
I lay dozens of eggs.
I have four shapely legs.
My sharp claws help me grip.
My long tail's like a whip.
I'm a lizard, by the way.
What's my name? Can you say?

j_____

My name has nine letters.
It starts with a J.
My long, dangling tentacles
capture my prey.
If my color is blue,
my sting will hurt you.
What can I possibly be?
Can you say?

k_____o

I start with a K and end with an O.
My strong hind legs
help me leap, fast or slow.
Through the air I can sail,
with my powerful tail.
From Australia I hail.
What am I? Do you know?

l_____g

I start with an L and end with a G.
I eat harmful insects.
Gardeners like me!
I have spots—at least two,
sometimes more, quite a few.
Lady's part of my name—
male or female, the same.
I'm a very small beetle.
Can you name me?

m_____y

I start with an M and end with a Y.
Find me in tall trees.
Hear my call, 'way up high.
I learn when I play,
and I play everyday.
The jungle's my gym,
and I really stay slim,
as I swing limb to limb.
Can you guess? What am I?

n_ _ _t

I start with a N and end with a T.
On water or land,
you'll recognize me.
I move like a fish,
side to side, swish-swish.
If it's warm, I dash about.
If it's cold, I just hang out.
I eat worms and bugs,
but I really like slugs.
  My skin's soft and slimy.
      What can I be?

O_____

I'm seven letters long
and start with an O.
I look for my food
on the sea bed below.
My eight arms help fetch
an abundant sea catch.
When danger's about,
I squirt black ink out,
and then safely, I go.
What am I? Do you know?

P_____

A rare sight to see, I start with a P.
If you do spot me,
you'll giggle with glee.
I toddle like a clown,
dressed in black,
and white down.
See my colorful beak
and you'll know I'm unique.
I'm a bird of the sea.
Can you name me?

q — — — —

I'm five letters long. I start with a Q.
I roam through the woods
and through grassy fields, too.
Bob-bob-white! I chatter
while my noisy wings clatter.
People hunt me for game.
Can you guess my name?

r_____

My name has ten letters.
It starts with an R.
I'm a very large mammal,
as big as a car.
I have very thick skin
and a very broad chin.
Funnel ears and tiny eyes
and big, thunder thighs!
I have two horns, or less.
What am I? Can you guess?

s___l

I start with an S and end with an L.
My body is wrapped
in a spiralling shell.
I crawl at a pace
much too slow for a race.
When I move, you can tell
by my trail of mucky jell.
What am I? Can you tell?

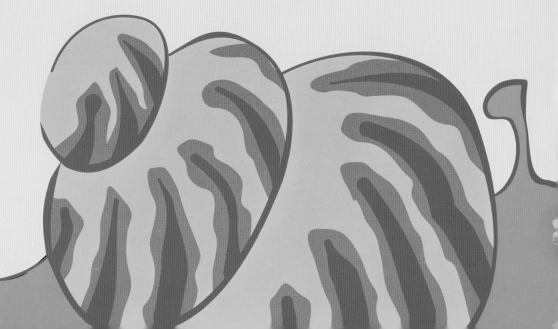

t_____

I'm six letters long
and start with a T.
I crawl across land,
or swim in the sea.
With four wrinkled legs,
I dig nests for my eggs.
I carry my home
wherever I roam.
(It's a most handsome dome!)
Can you name me?

___u

My name has three letters.
It ends with a U.
I'm a fast-running bird
and a good swimmer, too.
I have wings, but can't fly.
I stand two meters high.
Ba-ba-boom is my cry.
Can you guess who?

v__e

I start with a V and end with an E.
I'm soft and I'm furry,
but no one likes me.
I eat grass, seeds and roots.
I eat bark and plant shoots.
I eat all I find
and leave damage behind.
I hide underground
and am not often found.
It's hard to catch me.
What can I be?

w_____e

I start with a W and end with an E.
A magnificent mammal,
I live in the sea.
Catch me in action,
I'm quite an attraction.
I have flippers and a fin,
blubber's underneath my skin.
Please don't hunt me, let me be!
Can you guess? Can you name me?

_ _ X

I end with an X.
Find my tracks in the snow,
or along mountain trails,
or in valleys below.
I sleep most of the day.
At night, I hunt and play.
Chicken is my favorite meat,
but squirrel is a tasty treat.
People say I'm sly.
The fact is, I'm shy.
Do you know?
What am I?

y_____t

I start with a Y and end with a T.
I'm a wasp,
but I look like the sweet honeybee.
I have two pairs of wings
and give powerful stings.
My rather large nest
is made of wood—chewed and pressed.
Better beware of me! What can I be?

Z___U

I start with a Z and end with a U.
Find me in Africa, Asia, or the zoo.
My big horns curl around.
I make a *moo! moo!* sound.
My hump in clear view
and the way that I chew
give you more than one clue.
Bet you can't guess!
Do you know who?

ZZZZ

	iguana	rhinoceros
ant	jellyfish	snail
beaver	kangaroo	turtle
camel	ladybug	emu
duck	monkey	vole
elephant	newt	whale
firefly	octopus	fox
giraffe	puffin	yellowjacket
hippopotamus	quail	zebu

a_____l

I start with an A and end with an L.
I'm something that lives,
sometimes in a shell.
I breathe in and out
and I move about.
You know me well.
What am I? Can you tell?

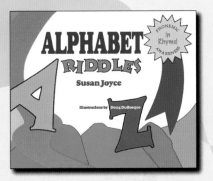

ALPHABET RIDDLES
Susan Joyce
Illustrations by Doug DuBosque
PHONEMIC Awareness in Rhyme!

If you've enjoyed this book, look for others,
including *Alphabet Riddles,* on our web site

http://peelbooks.com

or at your favorite bookseller

Ideas for Parents and Teachers

As a young child, I had dyslexia and had a difficult time reading, writing and speaking words. Fortunately, my parents believed that children can learn language lessons and be entertained at the same time. So as a family we played a word game we called alphabet riddles. We would make up riddles while riding in the car, or waiting on a bus, or whenever we felt bored, or had a few minutes to spare. It worked like magic! It made learning words fun!

Creating animal riddles that rhyme is a wonderful way to explore the world of words. As you engage children personally in the poetic process, you will see them blossom in their vocabulary, their understanding of words and their meanings. You will help them develop reading, writing, thinking and vocal presentation skills.

~ *Create animal riddles!* They don't have to be fancy. Choose an animal you like. Think of words that describe the animal. Begin with letter and word clues. Start with a simple riddle:

> *I start with an H and end with an E.*
> *I have a long face. What can I be?*

~ *Stretch the exercise.* Look the definition of the animal up in the dictionary. Read the definition aloud. Look at a picture of the animal. Add more lines, with more clues to the riddle.

~ *Share riddles!* Most written riddles can be solved independently, but it's always more fun to share a rhyming riddle. So, write it down and then share it with others.

~ *Instruct children to wait until all clues have been given* before guessing the riddle. Have the child who guesses the answer first say the correct word, spell it out, and then make up a new animal riddle.

~ Encourage children, as an extended activity, to *draw* the animal.

Have fun!

Susan Joyce